SIXPENNY WONDERFULS

6ᴰ gems from the past

Chatto & Windus/The Hogarth Press

Published in 1985 by
Chatto & Windus. The Hogarth Press
40 William IV Street
London WC2N 4DF

A PHOEBE PHILLIPS EDITIONS BOOK

British Library
Cataloguing in Publication Data
Sixpenny wonderfuls : 6d gems from the past.
1. Book covers – History – Pictorial works
2. Illustration of books – History – Pictorial
works
741.64   NC1882

ISBN 0-7011-3936-6

Printed in Yugoslavia

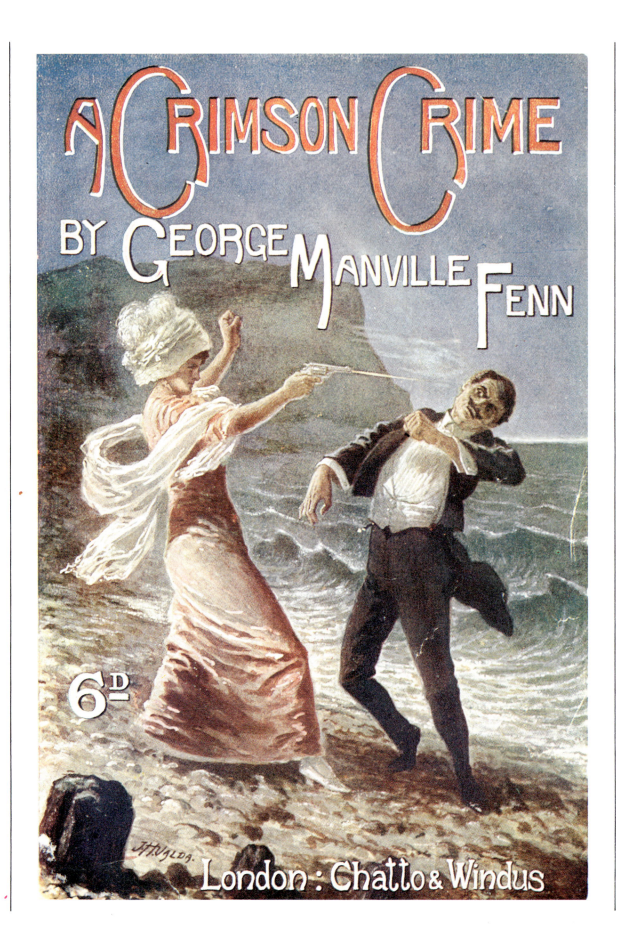

CONTENTS

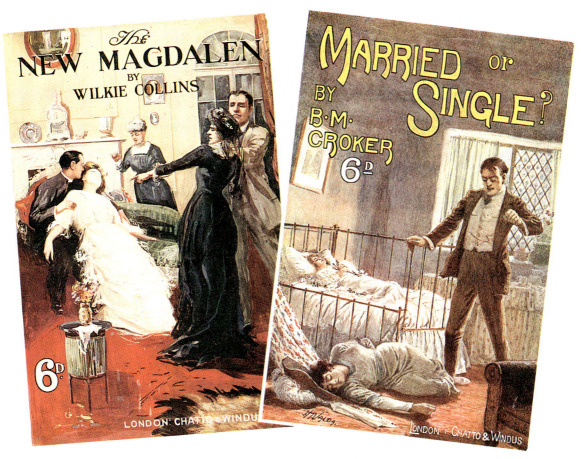

Introduction

"Only a novel! . . . in short, only some work in which the most thorough knowledge of human nature, the happiest delineations of its varieties, the liveliest effusions of wit and humour are conveyed to the world in the best chosen language . . ."

Jane Austen,
Northanger Abbey

Miss Austen, at least, had no doubts about the value of novels, but she was realistic enough to appreciate that all too many leaders of the literary world would have echoed "only a novel" rather than support her own more positive view.

Yet in spite of all the disapproval, story-telling proved far too popular to be ignored. By the 1870s, Charles Dickens, Wilkie Collins and other working journalists had already proved that books would sell to more than one market; hardbound, beautifully printed novels at 3s 6d were considered a luxury even by the comfortably situated middle class, but serialized novels in magazines and newspapers were wildly successful, reaching an audience that traditional publishers had barely considered.

Free schooling and libraries had encouraged a new, literate working class. Drifting away from rural villages to offices and factories in town, they worked long hours for little pay, but their free time was their own. Reading was a ticket to a different life, an exciting adventure or the promise of a bright future.

Chatto's directors were among the first publishers to move towards this new market. The intention was to republish some of their most successful hardbound novels in new, paper covers with bright colourful designs, and at a much cheaper price. The illustrators were commissioned to choose exciting and dramatic moments to attract the customers.

It must have been with a certain amount of trepidation that Chatto picked the first titles. *The Cloister and the Hearth* by Charles Reade had been selling in the thousands since 1861 when it was first published. Now, in 1893, the paperback print run was set at 50,000 copies, and in a few months it was clear the gamble had paid off handsomely. Within the next 15 years, an astonishing 380,000 copies were sold in the 6d. edition alone. Even in the first year, the reports were good enough for any publisher. The list of Chatto titles was searched for old novels or collections of light stories. There were a number of authors whose work seemed perfect for the new format; among them were parsons and vicars who were determined that books should have ethical value as well as enjoyment; writing novels themselves was one way to ensure that the contents would be acceptable as lessons in morality, and they turned them out in surprising numbers.

Sir Walter Besant was only one of another group of prolific writers who were ardent social reformers. Their books were also sermons in disguise, but this time preached with dedication against the abuses perpetrated by the late Victorian economy.

Not quite so seriously, Ouida and Mrs. Croker contributed romantic and light-hearted moments for relaxation, aimed at young women who dreamed of love and adventure though they themselves may never have travelled even to the centre of London, let alone to the deserts of Africa or the mountain passes of Australia.

The cover illustrations were sentimental but the actual texts were, by modern standards, very realistic. Young women were so hedged around with families and friends that for most, life began after marriage. So throughout the 6d. series passionate love affairs and romantic quarrels were written almost always about husbands and wives, although to be fair, they were not necessarily married to each other!

There were other writers who specialized in a different kind of adventure story. Emigration was increasing year by year as men and women left to make better lives in the colonies or with the great overseas trading companies. Suddenly the stories of jungle warfare or tribal ritual took on new meaning as the stuff of everyday life. Readers wanted authority and experience even from the novelists, and contemporary reviews of, for example, Bertram Mitford's books speak approvingly of "genuine knowledge" and "intimate understanding".

Another important part of the list had grown with Wilkie Collins. Chatto added detective novelists Manville Fenn and R. Austin Freeman to the 6ds; steeped in legal and medical jargon, they created the most realistic thrillers of their time.

India provided a canvas for adventure stories as well as exotic settings for romance. Mrs. Perrin and F.E. Penny wrote realistically about the growing problems of inter-racial marriage, but although the critics were enthusiastic, the sales show that a gloomier period was approaching. Ouida's books in her heyday had automatically sold over 100,000 copies; Mrs. Perrin's titles seldom reached an audience of more than 20,000.

During World War I, few titles were added to the list, except for the novels of Zola, which were also only moderately successful. But at the end of the war, in 1919, a great effort was made to revive the entire series. Old titles were republished and re-furbished with new covers, and other titles were bought in from outside publishers. All to no avail. Mrs. Croker's *The Cat's Paw* was published in an edition of 20,000; 18,000 were pulped ten years later. Even Ouida was clearly out of favour; *Princess Napraxine* was issued in 1912 with 25,000 copies as usual. In 1923 it was sadly noted in the records that 24,743 copies were still in the warehouses. Finally, in the 1920s and 1930s, the stacks were cleared, cover plates destroyed or melted down, and blocks were re-used, sold on to other publishers, or simply abandoned completely. For many of the titles, nothing remains but the covers.

Yet even today, these remain fascinating in themselves. A generation of readers is reflected in their dresses, their styles and their settings. They can still make us laugh and charm us with colour and vivacity and with decorative qualities — more permanent than their contents — which have lasted longer than their illustrators could have dared to hope, and far longer than the twenty or thirty years of Chatto's 6d. series.

We may know little or nothing about the artists, but a great deal about the world they show us, a few bright remnants of a brave experiment which was re-born only a few years later in the first Penguin paperbacks. Perhaps it is not so surprising that their price, too, was set at 6d, a small tribute to our own wonderful sixpennies.

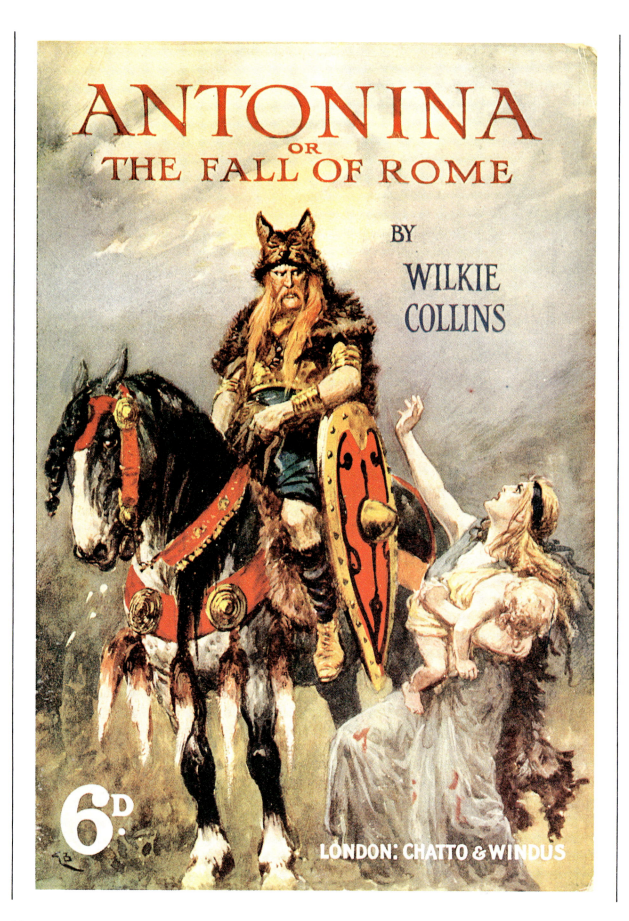

ANTONINA
OR
THE FALL OF ROME

BY
WILKIE COLLINS

6^D

LONDON: CHATTO & WINDUS

Looking Back

". . . it was an age in which artists sought out and loved one another . . ."

At the end of the nineteenth century, England was fascinated by the medieval world, and looked back through very deep rose-coloured glasses to a period which they plundered for clothes, furniture, architecture and painting.

Charles Reade (1814-84) was only one of the authors who found the Middle Ages a perfect setting for romance and adventure; this novel, reprinted in 1893, the first year of the 6d. editions, brought instant success to Chatto's new venture. The historical characters of **The Cloister and the Hearth** were as diverse as the High and Puissant Prince, Duke of Burgundy, and Gerard (later to be the father of Erasmus), a young calligrapher too poor to pay for gold leaf to illuminate his manuscripts. Reade could truthfully say that "he had told the story with human beings, and not through a population of dolls!" The public agreed, and bought an astonishing 380,000 copies.

This was quite in contrast to **Antonina or the Fall of Rome**, Wilkie Collins' (see p. 26) first book, re-printed the same year. The cover certainly promises well – a moment of barbaric drama complete with stern conqueror and weeping woman, yet poor Antonina went stumbling away from her horseman with the tears and sympathy of only 1,240 readers.

Mark Twain (1835-1910) also took a chance with history in **The Prince and the Pauper**, only moderately successful in this unillustrated version. None of Twain's novels really became popular in these cheaper editions, but they have outlasted most of their top-selling contemporary rivals.

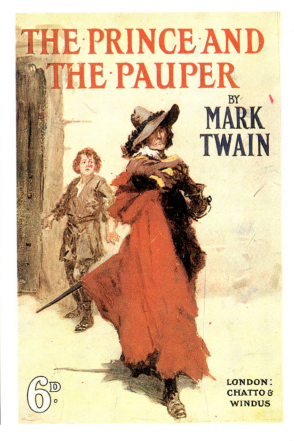

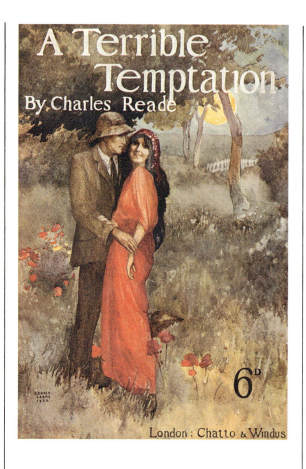

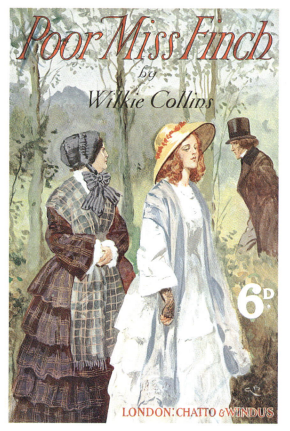

Country Manners

Village life, however simple, did have its scenes of romantic drama and excitement. The cottage setting of **Red Spider**, with its indignant sturdy girl in her homely apron, is both charming and attractive. Sabine Baring-Gould (1834-1924) was one of the many writing parsons whose output of tracts, articles and novels was nothing short of prodigious. **Red Spider** was published in 1887, and it was still being reprinted in 1904 – perhaps the medicine of moral admonition and warning went down best with a country setting (he was a rector in Devon) and lively characterization.

Charles Reade was a popular and dedicated social reformer; he wanted to show how appalling the law could be when it refused to acknowledge open abuse. **A Terrible Temptation** is based on how the inheritance law tempted poor relatives to conspiracy and even crime in pursuit of wealth. Not surprisingly, the 6d. cover artist in 1907 decided a sultry love scene would be much more tempting to the reader, as the scheming young cousin tries to discredit and disinherit the rightful heir.

Poor Miss Finch has no belligerent village lad to clench fists outside her door. Wilkie Collins wrote lighter stories as well as the mysteries for which he is known. He knew the middle-class world well; his modest and well-brought-up heroine wouldn't dream of acting too independently, but she was perfectly capable of bringing the young man up to scratch when the time came, no matter how indifferently he chose to walk by her down the country lane.

RED SPIDER

By
S. Baring-Gould

6D

LONDON
CHATTO & WINDUS

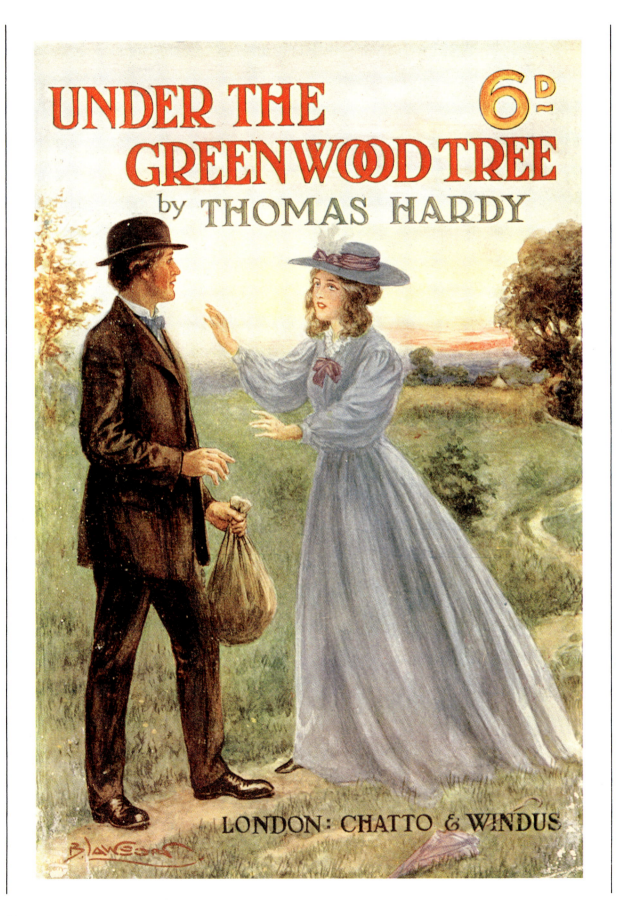

A Rural Idyll

"I be sure of one thing; no new-fangled instrament is going to sound out on Master's birthday, no matter what Vicar says."

There is a sense of proportion in Hardy's Dorset, where love and passion take their place as only a part of rural life. To the village choir, whose leader is quoted above, Fancy the schoolmistress's love affair is much less important than the Vicar's new harmonium. Nonetheless, the illustrator for the cover knew that the young couple made a more attractive picture than a musical 'instrament'.

Under the Greenwood Tree is Thomas Hardy's (1840-1920) first book and one of his most delightful evocations of the countryside. Such country matters – the slow pace, the crisis in the village hall, the confrontation under the lych gate and the gentle charms of a country lane – were blissfully innocent compared to the preoccupations of crusading preachers who thundered against the perils of cities and their drinking and gambling houses.

Of course, all was not perfect in this simple world of the plough and the harvest, but the rural poor seldom went walking in a top hat – no wonder D. Christie Murray's heroine is so startled. A curious fact – **Joseph's Coat** was also the name of a popular riding cloak for ladies, certainly not illustrated here!

Rural scenes, with their green settings and romantic innocence, remained popular throughout the years. The young lovers in **Infatuation** could be characters in any of these novels; only their clothes put them clearly into this century.

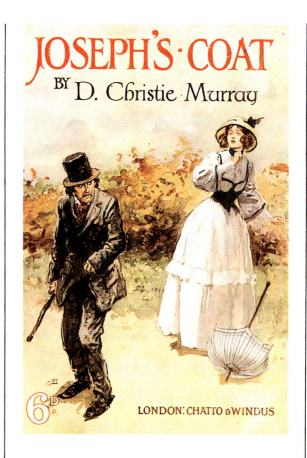

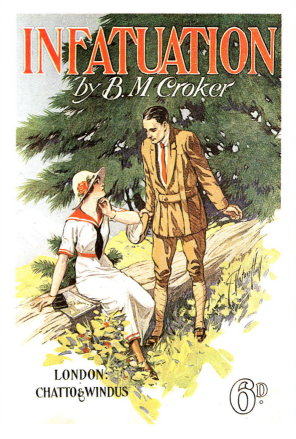

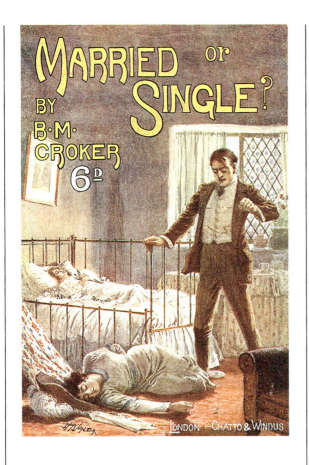

City Marriages

"She blenched at his dissolute look, his wretched clothes, the sheen on his fine-bred face now lined and soured in hate."

In spite of all their efforts to reach the state of marriage for both hero and heroine, writers and readers alike knew this was only the beginning. Romantic Victorian novelists were not blind to the realities of married life – far from it. The plots usually feature newly-weds subject to all the temptations of a busy city life. They came to terms with marriage in considerable discomfort, young mothers dying and children crying, drunken husbands and tyrannical parents, scheming friends and mistaken loyalties . . .

Here, two wives have been caught in a trap, the first innocently, the second in a web of her own weaving.

Frank Barrett's heroine will suffer unless her husband dies or reforms. Mrs Croker's heroine is more tarnished. She leaves her poor but upright husband and child to lead a life of apparent frivolity. Her child dies. However, true repentance earns her reprieve, as well as her husband's love again, *and* her inheritance too!

Mrs Croker was a prolific contributor to the 6d. series. She never reached the notoriety or success of Ouida, but her books sold consistently well from the 1890s to the 1920s, when the entire series suffered a sharp decline.

The Martyrdom of Madeline epitomizes the sophisticated lure of high living. Robert Buchanan (see p. 30) was quick to point out that maid servants in uniform and idle luxury were poor prescriptions for a happy wife.

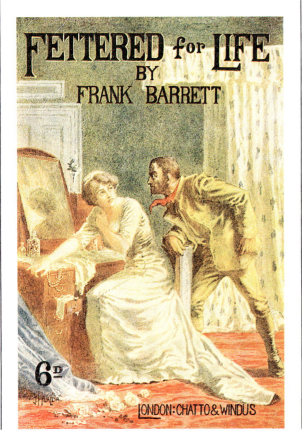

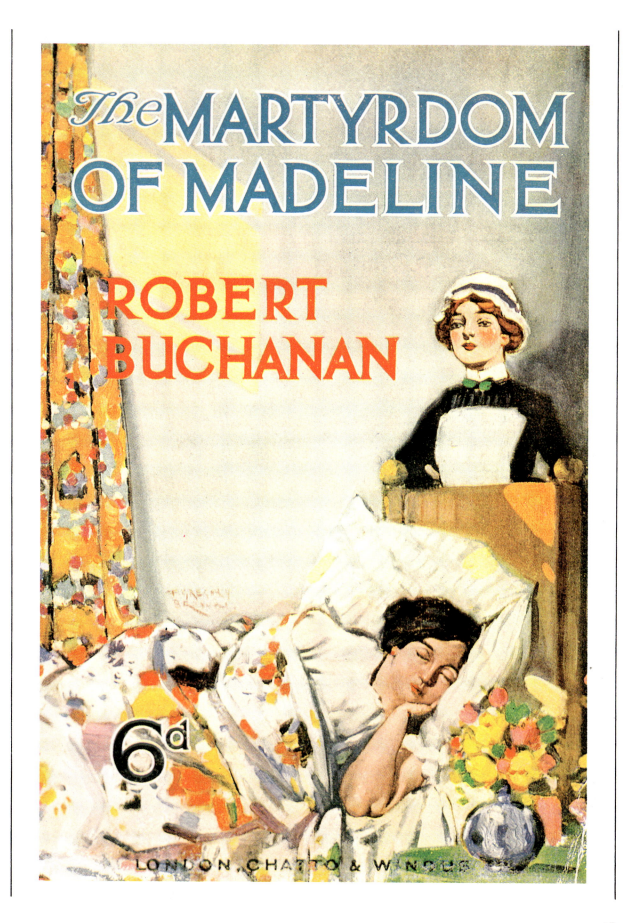

The Eavesdropper

"She saw them – ah, how *could* she see through her tears – her husband in the arms of that woman . . ."

That an eavesdropper learns what is best left hidden is an old truth, but where would the romantic novelist be without this useful device?

Careful plotting could bring a character to the scene of any appropriate incident, and the dramatic result would ensure that the figure in the shadows as well as the reader would be shocked and preferably dismayed, outraged and deeply hurt, at the same time.

Of course, pleasantly often it was a false alarm and all would be well.

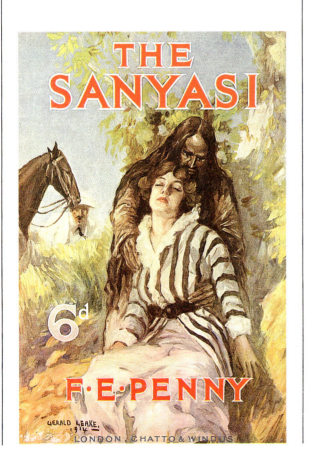

But not always – to S. Baring-Gould (see p. 12) any woman could be a temptress, a veritable **Eve**, betraying the trust and confidence of her husband.

Mistaken identity, misunderstandings, this moment of high drama appears over and over again, in novels with settings as far apart as the Vicarage in **Foxglove Manor** and the deepest jungle of **The Sanyasi.** Yet the settings are not as different as they seem; F.E. Penny was quite at home in Buchanan's vicarage; he was the Reverend Frank Penny, Madras Service Rtd!

"He covered his eyes, reeled back with a sob rising in his throat, and fled for the sanity of simple soldiering . . ."

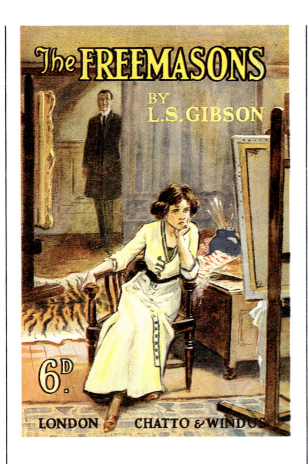

Unwilling Lambs

Ouida's novels sold poorly in the expensive editions, but **Strathmore**, first published in 1885, eventually reached over 100,000 faithful readers. The unprotected and frightened young girl dependent on the ambitious or cruel older man was, and is, a fruitful source of material, still found today in stories and novels.

"I have kept you as my own, when I need not have kept you half so well."

Margaret Cross chose a more unusual subject, one which was all too real, but seldom acknowledged. The orphan's fate, to be financially dependent on a guardian, was common enough when so many women died early in childbirth, and men left their families to serve their country abroad, or to make their fortunes in the colonies. The scrupulous step-parent would do his best, but when finances were strained, even such a man might be tempted. Then the mere presence of the child could become a reproach, and the cover shows just such a moment.

Then there were the stories in which innocence is confronted by secret dangers; we cannot see what has made the young girl so apprehensive on the cover of **The Freemason**, but her expression is enough to remind us of Ouida's frightened heroine in Strathmore, and it shows how freemasons were regarded with fear and suspicion, an attitude which has crept into our own time with the same lack of factual evidence.

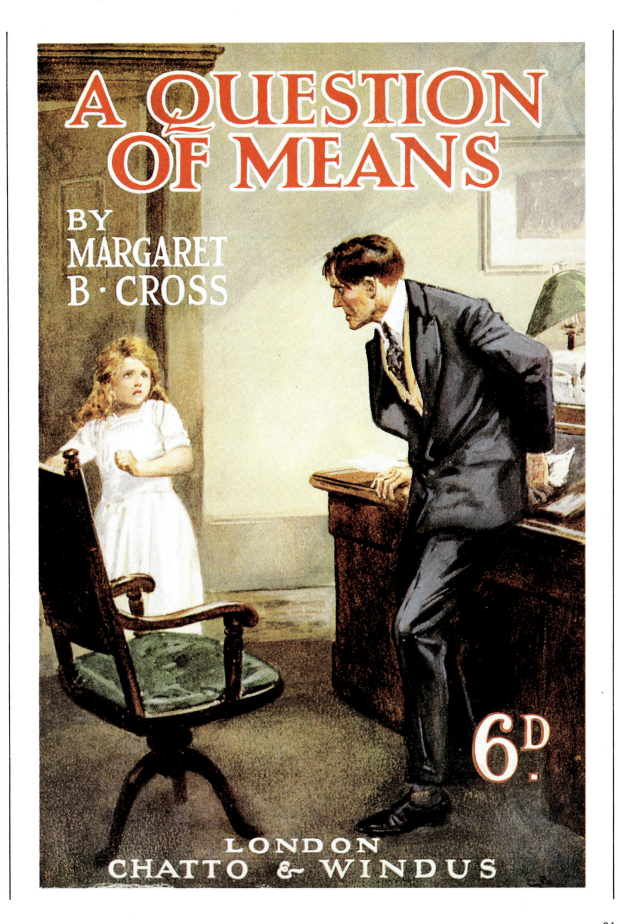

A QUESTION OF MEANS

BY
MARGARET
B·CROSS

6D.

LONDON
CHATTO & WINDUS

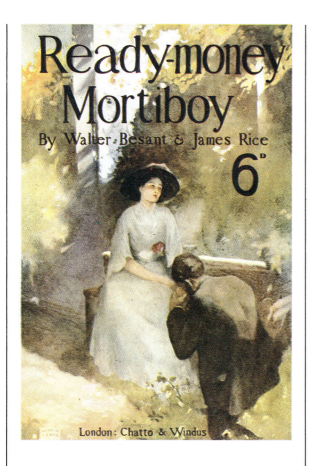

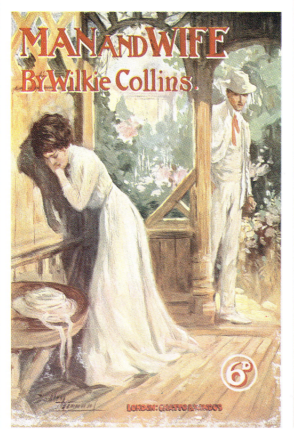

"Of all pleasant things upon the earth, there comes an end in time. Nay, the more pleasant are the things, the shorter they are and the faster they hasten away. This is wisely ordained lest we forget in the present the joys which await us . . . " The heroine of **Ready-Money Mortiboy** looks on the cover as far from the happiness of this world as the author could have wished.

Walter Besant (1836-1901) was a well-known writer of his time, whose novels were often laced with strong injunctions to consider the frivolity of earthly life. His early, lighter stories were written with James Rice (1843-82), a journalist remembered only for his collaboration with Besant. Sir Walter, as he became, continued to write even more about the social reforms which he championed, although he drew the line at any political power for women. He founded the Society of Authors in 1884, a much more lasting service to literature than his books.

Ouida's heroine in **Moths** appears equally aware of our temporary existence on this earth, and just as miserable as the future Mrs Mortiboy, but she was miserable with considerably more style. Needless to say, Sir Walter did not approve of Ouida and her very unconventional ideas, and her success must have been mortifying (see p. 24).

Wilkie Collins shows another face of sorrow and repentance; the young husband seems abashed by his wife's tears in the summerhouse. There were many romances such as **Man and Wife**, about a couple who may have met only a few times before their marriage, and whose first years were spent learning to know each other, the woman in particular discovering the mysteries and difficulties of a sexual relationship.

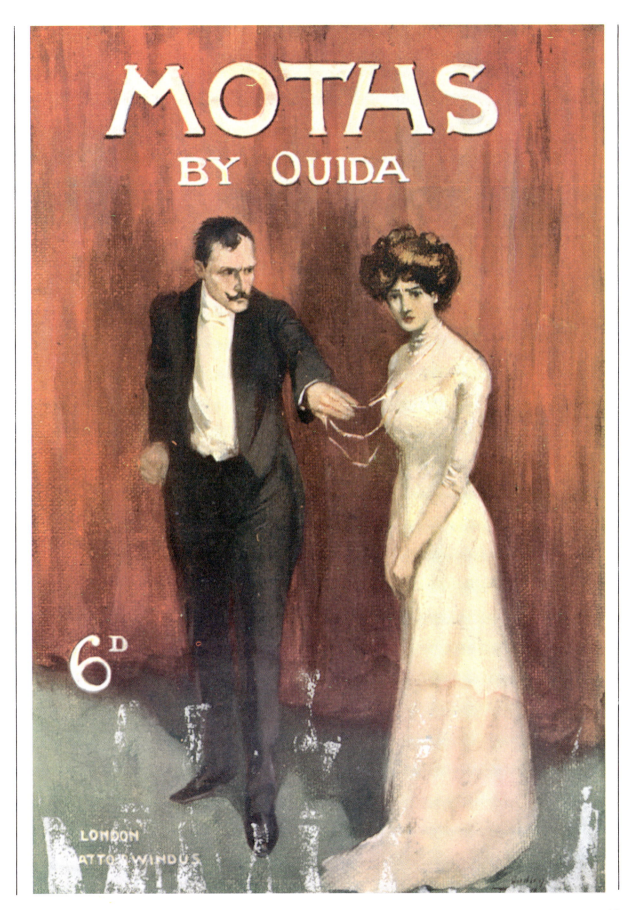

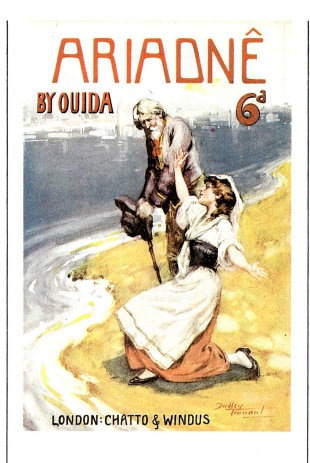

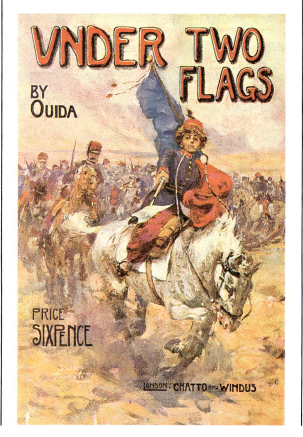

Ouida Alone

"Let us go now. There is nothing left but chance."

There is no question but that Marie Louis de la Ramée (1839-1908) was a phenomenon. Born in the very English town of Bury St. Edmunds to a French father and an English mother, for all her prolific career she wrote about exotic characters and places that were a very long way from her respectable Suffolk birthplace.

In her early short stories and novels she developed a style of passionate and fast-moving narrative that covered all the gaps in her rather limited knowledge of the French Foreign Legion, Gypsy life, Arabian tents, and so on.

Although many of the more literary pundits laughed at her mistakes and overheated plots, the public bought – and bought – and bought. Chatto printed over 200,000 copies of many titles in the cheaper editions, and even published an anthology called "The Wit and Wisdom of Ouida."

She died just before her popularity and her previously loyal readers dropped away almost to nothing. **Ariadnê** and **Under Two Flags** were typical of her early adventurous successes, but by the time the more sophisticated **Puck** was reprinted in 1919 at 9d., it failed completely and almost the whole edition was pulped. "She watched her entire world die, just as the light in her own eyes was dimming gradually to the shadows of lifelessness" might have been her own epitaph.

A Remarkable Man

Victorian fiction is replete with names and titles which have vanished from popular knowledge, but William Wilkie Collins (1824-89), a mainstay of the 6d. editions, will always be known for two great classics of mystery and detection, **The Moonstone** and **The Woman in White.** Collins was the son of a well-known painter, but instead of being sympathetic to his literary ambitions, Mr Collins tried to steer his son into business and law. Although it didn't stop Wilkie from becoming a writer, this early education was to be very useful.

By the time Collins was 27, he had already written **Antonina** (p.10), and become a friend and collaborator of Charles Dickens, but it wasn't until the serialization of **The Woman in White** in 1859 and **The Moonstone** in 1868 that

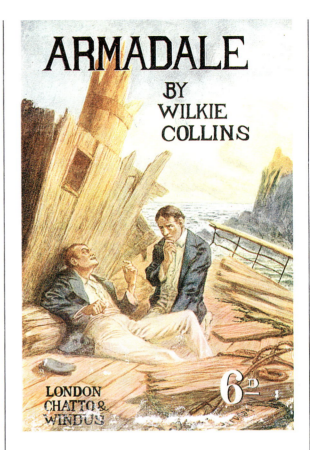

his name became well known to the popular press. Each sold over 100,000 copies in their first year at 6d. (1895 and 1896, respectively), confirming his reputation.

Perhaps unfortunately, these two titles have remained so familiar in film and television as well as in print, that the rest of his work, like **Armadale**, **The Dead Secret** and **No Name**, has almost vanished from print. They are all still well worth reading for their vivid, if sometimes lengthy picture of contemporary life; often the covers depict the dramatic confrontation, the moment of horror so beloved of all Victorian readers.

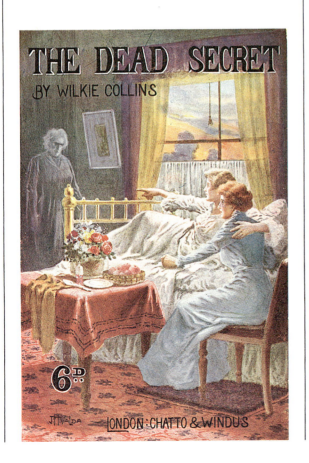

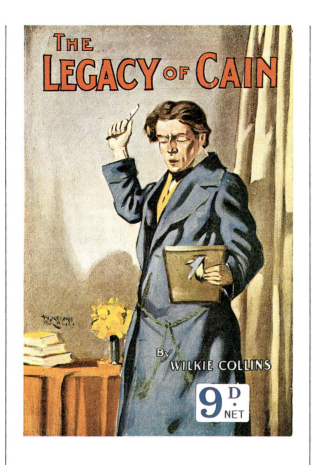

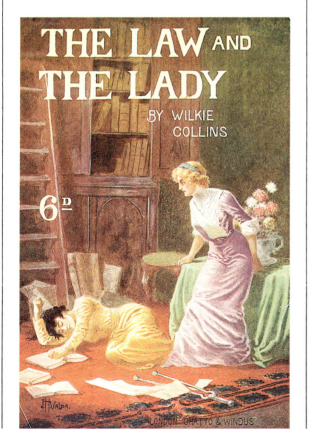

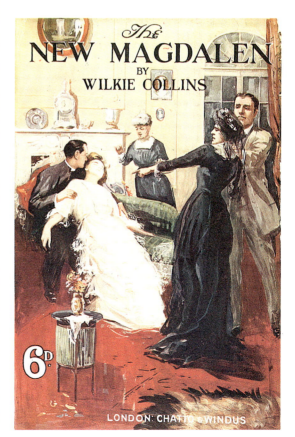

THE MOONSTONE

BY
WILKIE COLLINS

6^D

J.M.VALDA

LONDON: CHATTO & WINDUS.

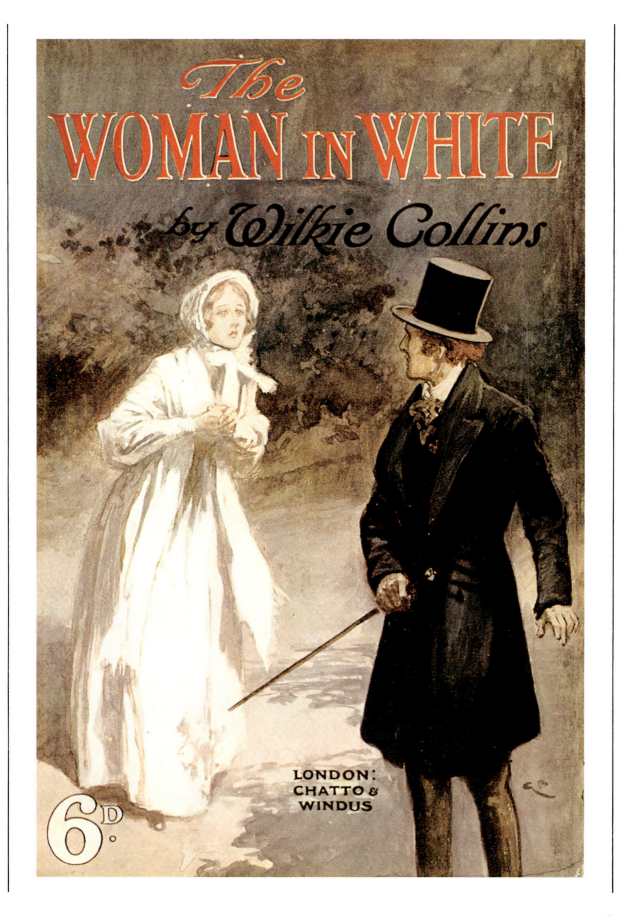

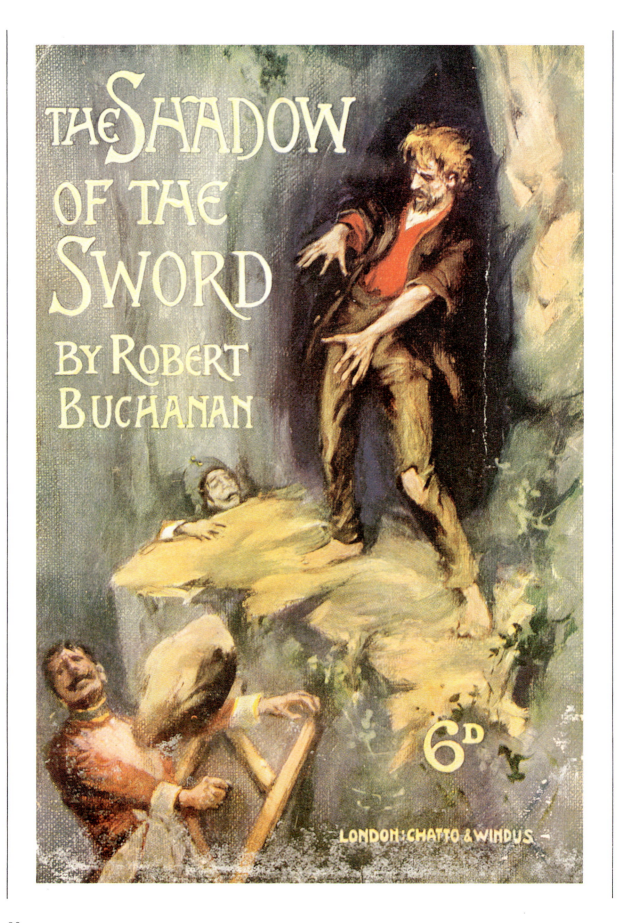

THE SHADOW OF THE SWORD

BY ROBERT BUCHANAN

6D

LONDON: CHATTO & WINDUS

Shadows in the Dark

". . . there are shadows in all our lives, but some have shadows which move in the darkness of their minds, forever . . ."

Premonitions? Mute accusers of past misdeeds? The greedy and mysterious influence which we can never quite see clearly . . . shadows of every description were a favourite theme in late Victorian novels.

Sir Thomas Henry Hall Caine (1838-1931) wrote novels set in the Cumberland hills and the countryside of the Isle of Man, where he grew up. **The Deemster** was a considerable success; though it was not republished in the 6d. series until 1903, it sold over 100,000 copies. Caine understood the enormous value of financial independence, and the overwhelming need for money in a poorly developed rural area shadowed the lives of most of his characters. His books sold year after year, although they are seldom read nowadays.

Today he is remembered more for his friendship with D. G. Rossetti, and for one of his plays which featured the young Compton Mackenzie. Mackenzie wrote that Caine was as dour and pessimistic in character as the countryside around his home.

Robert William Buchanan (1841-1901), poet, writer and socialist, was equally committed to the right of every man to carve a place for himself in society, using swords of righteousness as well as the shadows of greed and crime. He was a very serious man, but like many fellow journalists he wrote dozens of novels in every kind of setting.

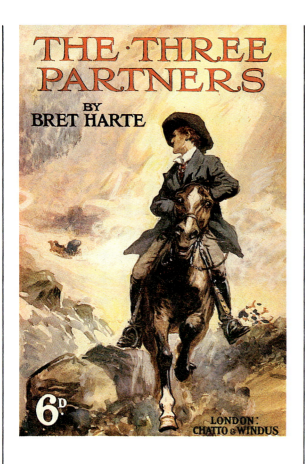

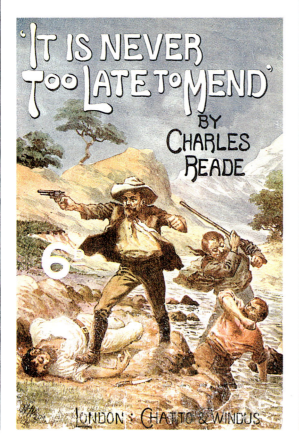

To many of his English readers, Francis Bret Harte (1836-1902) was the American West incarnate. His stories and ballads were widely hailed as the true voice of the pioneer. Harte had lived in San Francisco for a time, and worked as a journalist and short story writer; his best and earliest work reflected that time of his life – vivid imagery, crisp dialogue and landscapes where the sage brush simply rolled away to the wide horizons. It was not all dust and poverty, either; the rider shown on the cover of **The Three Partners** is an elegant horseman.

Harte went on to be a gold prospector, a Wells Fargo rider, and in the true outlaw-turned-marshal tradition, a government official. But after he moved to Europe and became US consul in such cities as Glasgow, London and Berlin, the old spirit of the West died away, and his later work never recaptured that authentic atmosphere.

The Golden Butterfly is set in a typical desert landscape, though neither of its authors (see p. 22) had, as far as we know, ever met an Indian squaw. Yet their book sold over 130,000 copies in five years; more than ten times as many as Harte's.

Australia was another new world, and Charles Reade (see p. 12) used the terrible conditions of mining towns and convict workhouses to write the first "reforming" novel (1856), working with fiction to portray social problems, which was re-published in 1896 with respectable success.

Cowboys and Little Boys

English readers were fascinated by the special atmosphere of freedom, excitement and danger of the open range.

In Arizona, Mississippi or Queensland, the land was a prize that could only be won with the hard work of your own hands. There was not much of a traditional judicial system to get in the way of an ambitious rancher or cowboy. A man could do what a man had to do, as Florence Warden's **Tom Dawson** personifies. There's no mistaking his self-possession or his heroic stance! Yet, surprisingly, the truly American Mark Twain, the pseudonym of Samuel Clemens (1835-1910), never quite reached the popular audience so anxious to read about cowboys and Indians, cowhands and sheep herders.

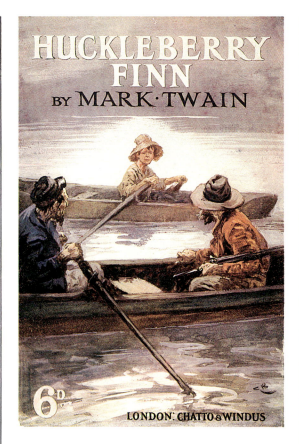

The gentle fun and experiences of the young heroes may have been just a little too American for popularity, or the 6d. price too high at the time for a book apparently written for children.

Both **Huckleberry Finn** and **The Adventures of Tom Sawyer** were printed only once, in 1904, and never reprinted for this series.

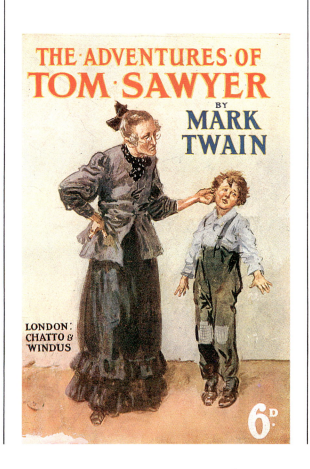

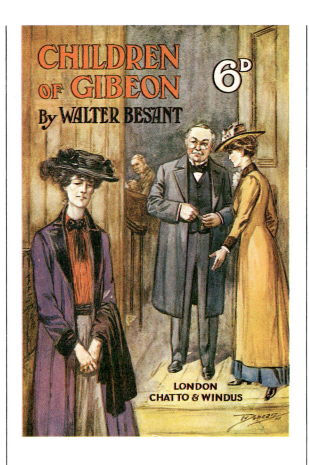

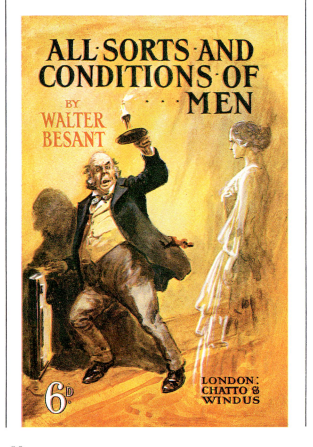

Moral and Amoral

Sir Walter Besant (see p. 22) cared deeply about social conditions in London. He planned a set of guides to London, and had been particularly horrified by conditions in the East End when he was researching his text.

These two novels, **All Sorts and Conditions of Men** and **The Children of Gibeon**, were almost straight propaganda for his great cause, persuading the public to support his energetic campaign for a People's Palace in Mile End, to provide amusement and education in an area where these were almost unknown.

Mrs Margaret Hungerford (1855-97) was equally well known at the time for *not* letting her social conscience dominate her novels, even though she was a canon's daughter! The Saturday Review said of **A Modern Circe** that "Mrs Hungerford is a distinctly amusing author; in all her books there is a healthy absenteeism of ethical purpose."

She wrote at least twenty novels, but in spite of their completely opposite intentions, she and Sir Walter share the common fate of being largely unread today. "She pictured herself fifty years from now, unknown, un-cared for, but not unendowed with wealth. She sighed for the world's praises that were not to be, and settled down to a very comfortable future with a smile."

A·MODERN·CIRCE

By the Author of
"MOLLY BAWN"

6D.

LONDON:
CHATTO & WINDUS

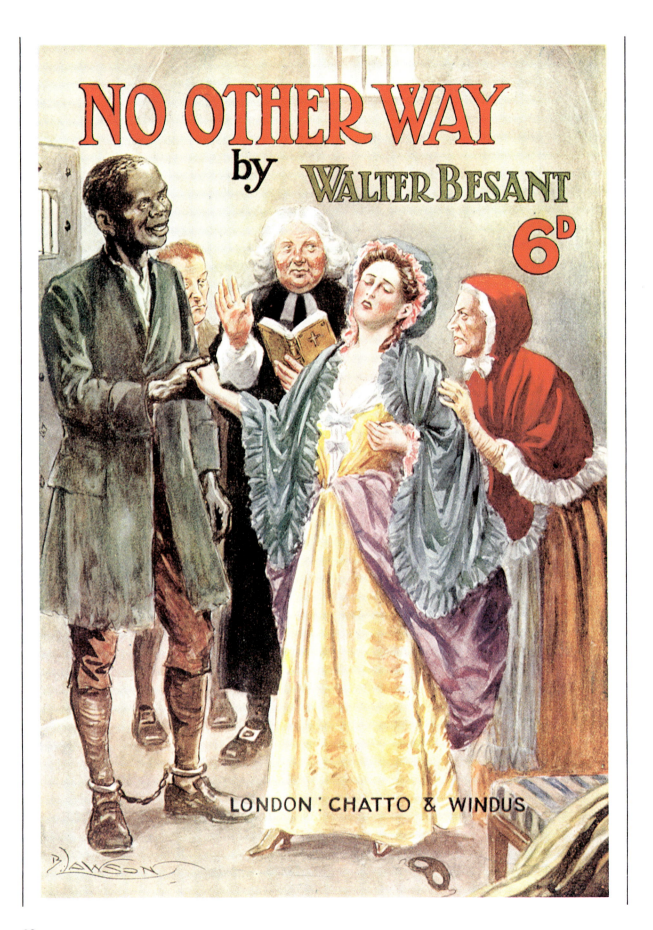

Reformers All

"No matter what it cost, a man's dignity cannot be traduced in this fashion. Let it take all my reputation, I will see it through . . ."

The need to press for social reform through the popular press did not seem to abate. Sir Walter's **No Other Way** in its rather heavy-handed presentation makes it clear that the official abolition of slavery in 1802 had not necessarily convinced the average reader.

Although the cover could not have done very much to persuade parents or friends of delicate young ladies like the heroine that her sacrifice would be worthwhile, it clearly shows that writers were willing to tackle some of the most controversial problems in late Victorian society.

The "jolly jack tar" was much nearer the ordinary English heart. W. Clark Russell (1844-1911) had served in the Merchant Navy for eight years, and in addition to his straightforward biography of Lord Nelson, he wrote at least 50 sea-stories which portrayed some of the terrible conditions still considered acceptable, and these led to many quiet reforms within the Service. The passage of convicts to Australia, and the behaviour of men who had to care for them on board, was another issue, and Russell attempted to suggest a better balance between humanity and punishment.

Eliza Lynn Lynton (1822-98) was married to an ardent reformer, and shared his views, but her novels successfully hid them from the reader.

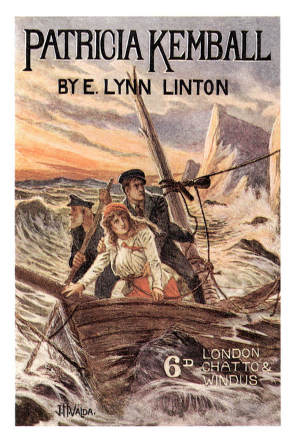

Le Maître

Social reform wasn't confined to crusaders on one side of the English Channel. Émile Zola (1840-1902) was possessed of the same zeal for obliterating abuses and moral indignities as his contemporaries.

Zola became involved in a huge project to show the effects of hereditary disease and social decay on a single family, traced through the generations. **Germinal** and **The Fortune of the Rougons** were both books from the series. **Germinal** was based on the difficult life of coal-miners in north-west France, and this would have been well understood by the English workers in Wales and the Midlands. *Nana*, another title in the same group, has remained popular even today in many 'classics' editions, but earlier in the century its theme of prostitution was

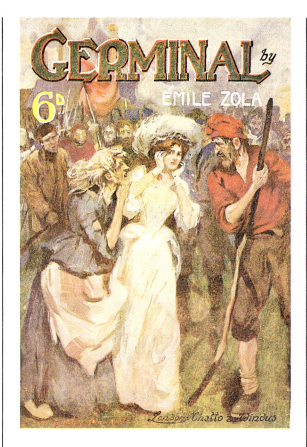

considered too immoral for popular readership, and it was not included in the 6d. publications.

The lust for **Money** and the effects of alcoholism were obviously more suitable subjects, and Zola's almost violently anti-clerical and anti-Catholic leanings were also heartily acceptable to an English audience still suspicious of Popery.

These very effective book covers are different in style from many of the Chatto novels, and they express their themes with restrained atmosphere. The 6d. editions were published around 1911-14, and most of the covers were drawn by Gerald Leake.

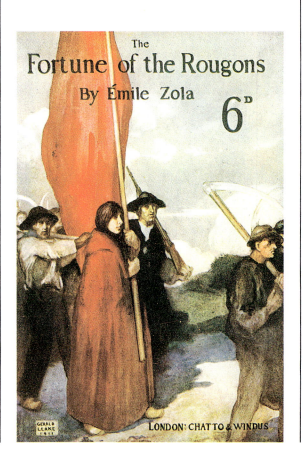

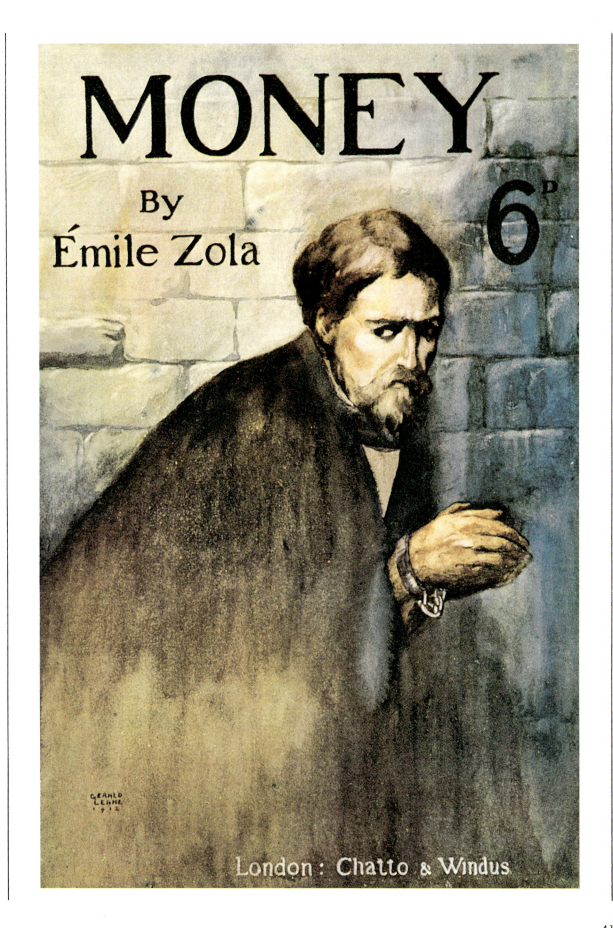

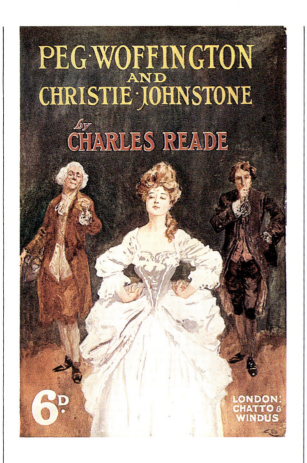

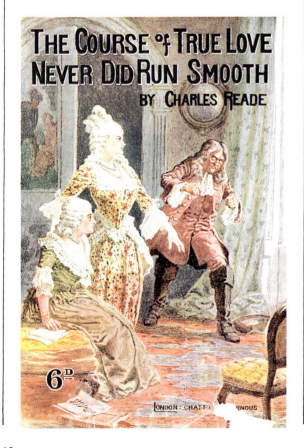

Entertainments

Even reformers weren't serious all the time; Charles Reade (see p. 12) was always fascinated by the stage, and most of his first literary attempts were plays or stories about the theatre. It took him a long time to achieve any success, until **Masks and Faces** was followed in 1853 by a novel about David Garrick, **Peg Woffington and Christie Johnstone**, which sold almost 100,000 copies between 1893, its first 6d. printing, and 1902. **The Course of True Love** was an obvious sequel, and both the stories and the settings are as extravagantly 18th century as the author and the illustrator can provide.

A different kind of entertainment was provided by the **New Arabian Nights,** a delightful group of tales by Robert Louis Stevenson (1850-94).

The cobbled street, the sympathetic young maid and the distressed young man – all the ingredients for a story that is just about to begin. But the expensive edition was not successful – only 500 copies were printed – and even the 6d. edition did not sell as well as expected. Stevenson is probably best known for his children's books *Treasure Island* and *Kidnapped.* He travelled all his life, sending stories and novels back from Belgium, California, France – wherever he happened to be.

High Society

By the turn of the century, many readers who saved regularly for their 6d. novel had left domestic service and rural employment behind. They thronged to the city, to factories, offices and workshops, far from the homes and daily life of the wealthy aristocracy. So the books and their covers became their only real source of information about High Society.

The authors responded with scenes set in fine houses or hotels, with beautiful jewels and elegant clothes described in detail, and with stories of success for people who could now dream of aiming as high as growing ambition would take them. One dressmaker in a respectable but not fashionable part of London was known to have copied clothes from the illustrations of popular novels to please her clients.

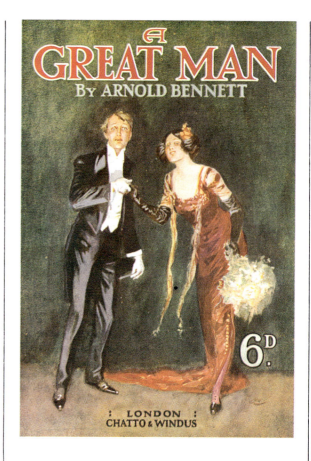

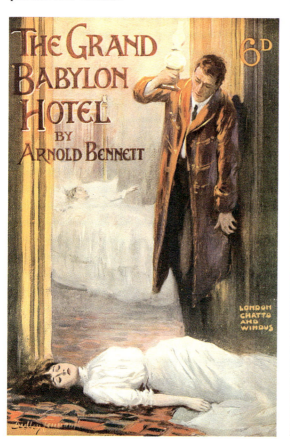

Arnold Bennett (1867-1931) was a superb storyteller, and although best known now for his evocative books about the Potteries (the *Clayhanger* series) he was happy to turn occasionally to a different scene, and a different atmosphere. The extravagant clothes and rich colours of **A Great Man** and his well-known **The Grand Babylon Hotel** were guaranteed to please an audience thirsty for detail – **Hotel** in particular sold year after year, and the serial rights were sold to Norway, Denmark, Germany and France – a real coup for publisher and author. Max O'Rell is unknown today, except for a strange collection of stories called **Rambling in Womanland**, but every touch in the cover for **Her Royal Highness, Woman** speaks of life a long way above stairs.

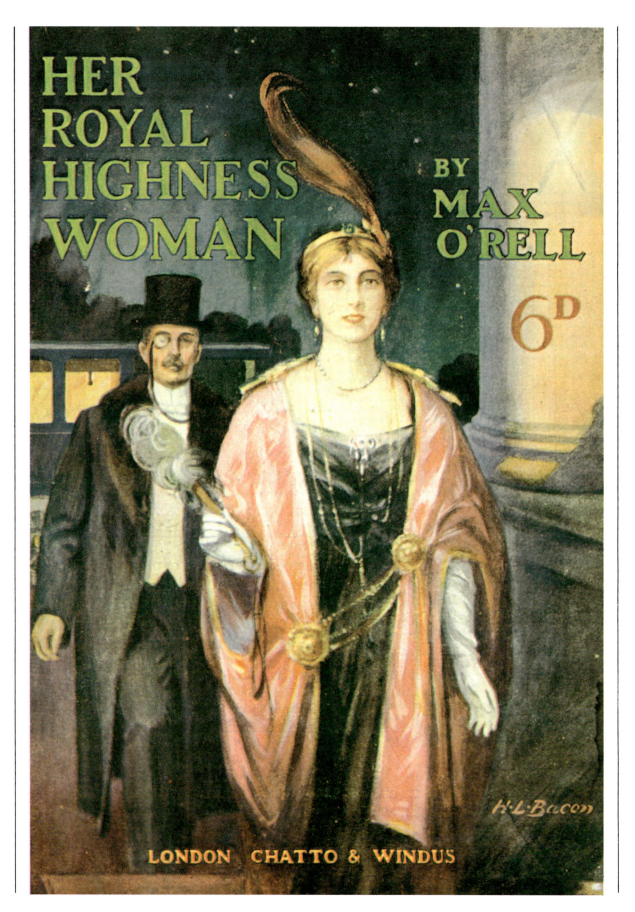

HER
ROYAL
HIGHNESS
WOMAN

BY
MAX
O'RELL

6D

LONDON CHATTO & WINDUS

A Cultivated Man

Arnold Bennett's entertaining stories were one of the main contributions to the success of the 6d. novels.

Like many of his fellow writers, he had originally intended to become a solicitor, but a few published articles persuaded him to try writing and journalism. However, Bennett did not turn to the kind of social and reforming literature which was so prominent at the period, but wrote short stories for magazines, including the famous *Yellow Book*, and then became assistant editor of *'Woman'* in 1893, writing everything from fashion commentary to cookery and social news. This experience was to make his books immensely popular with women – he

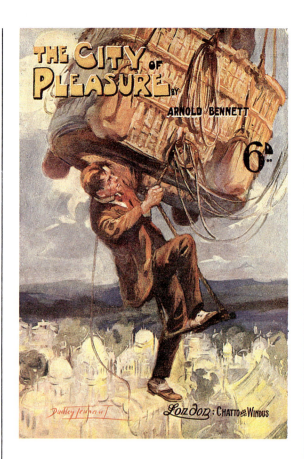

got so much domestic detail exactly right, and he knew how to interest and amuse the reader with the first few sentences – but he also wrote articles and editorials for many more academic publications.

The covers of these particular novels reflect the sophistication of fashionable London (see p. 44). He was highly regarded as a host, a man of taste (his paintings included a Bonnard and a Signac) and a remarkable reporter; his *Journals* are a truly fascinating account of his life and the world he lived in.

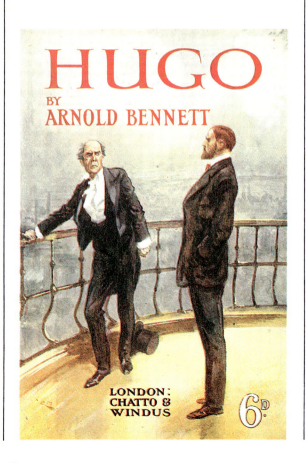

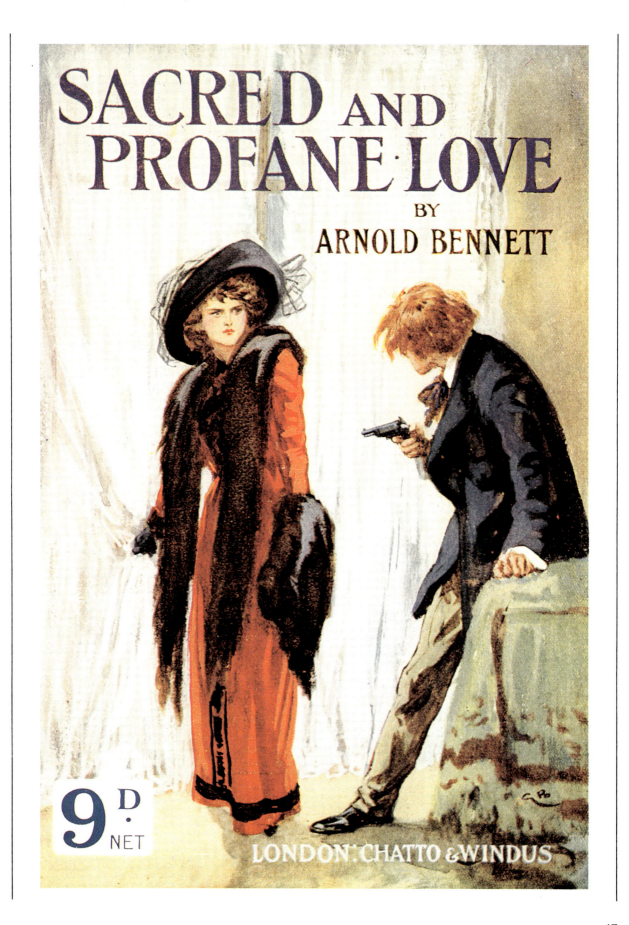

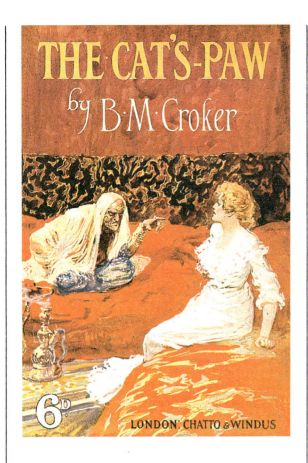

"How dare you! And I another female!"

Helpless femininity was often depicted as the appropriate source of womanly power, and even Mrs Croker and Ouida, defenders of women's right to independence, clung to plots in which women challenged each other only over men, marriage or society.

So these books are unusual in depicting only women on the cover; there is no lurking male figure, even in the background, to take attention from the combatants.

Mrs Croker is represented here by **The Cat's-Paw**, one of her more exotic settings, with a dramatic warning from a fortune teller or soothsayer. Ouida is more subtle; two rivals in her **Princess Napraxine** clash in their style of dress and period as well as in their passion.

But there is no real contest for effectiveness: the amazing illustration on the cover of **Paris** has the most verve and appeal. **Paris** is one of a trio of Émile Zola's late novels, intended to show the effects of religious and social customs of everday life. Most of his novels (see p. 40) had quiet, serious covers, but this one has somehow inspired the illustrator to a magnificent *tour de force*.

Here, Madame and her servant are engrossed in their private quarrel, the violence implied by the about-to-be-flung roses is perfectly judged, and the setting is everything that is French and upper middle class: a classical statue, gilded chairs and tables, even the striped wallpaper and moulded fireplace, a superb foil for the determined redhead. "How dare you!" indeed.

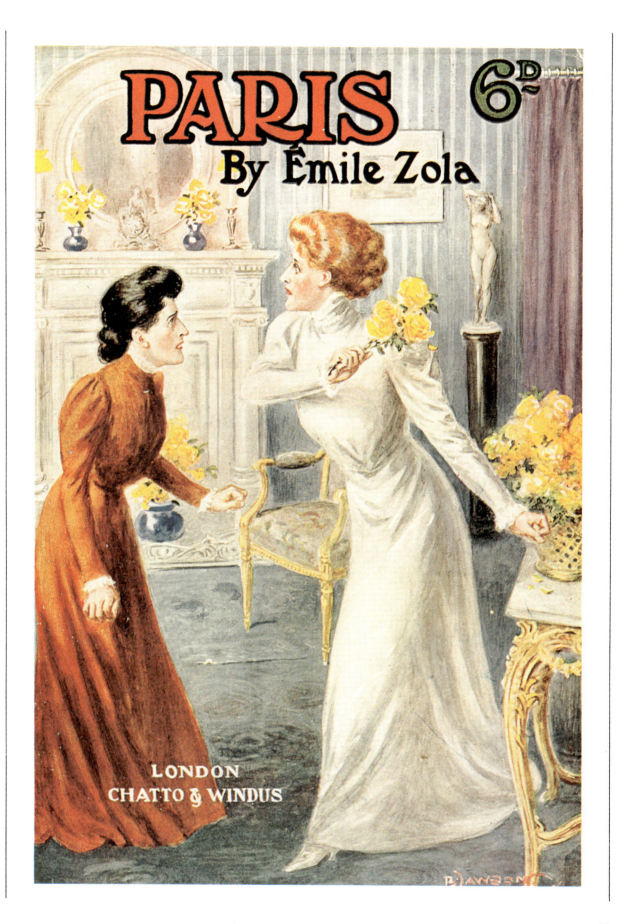

Ladies on Horseback

Another refreshing change from fainting maidens and well-chaperoned modesty, this trio of adventurous riders gallop along with all the dash of a new era.

"The freedom, the wind, the right to go where she chose, when she chose – was there ever a greater liberator than a horse?"

Perhaps the covers owe something to the fact that although all three novels date from the 1880s, they were republished in the 1920s during a last attempt to revive the popular cheap editions with new artwork and a modern approach.

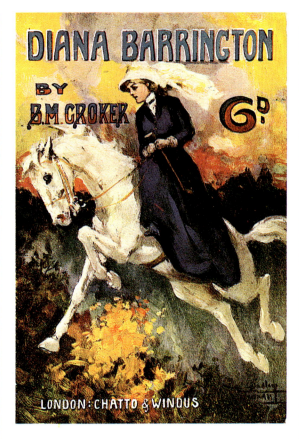

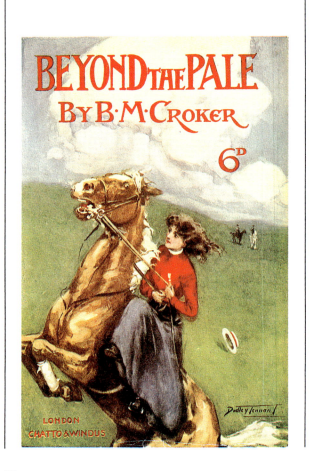

The two Croker girls were repainted for the later editions. **Diana Barrington** and **Beyond the Pale** had first appeared in 1897 and 1899 respectively; unfortunately the earlier illustrations have vanished – we know only that these two new ones cost £5.10s. each in 1923. Not perhaps a wise investment. **Diana** had sold well over 50,000 in the late 1890s, but only 759 copies of the 1923 edition were sold.

The MISTRESS OF BONAVENTURE

By
HAROLD
BINDLOSS

6D.

LONDON : CHATTO & WINDUS

The Domestic Heroine

"Well, what are we going to do now? The maids have left, Cook's having a tantrum, and my new dress has been sat on by the dogs . . ."

One would think that was enough to daunt any cheerful soul, but not George Robert Sims' heroine **Mary Jane.** Sims (1847-1922) was remarkable in creating realistic domestic scenes for his comedies, which were deservedly popular with hundreds of thousands of readers. **Mary Jane**, married or single, was an escape from zeal, tragedy and reform. The girls were laughing most of the time, and managed to maintain a sense of fun and enjoyment when most authors would have been tempted to moralize, or at the very least send them off to Africa or Arabia to

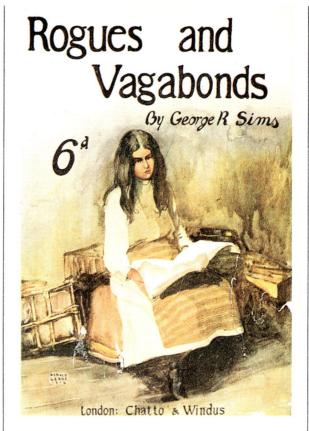

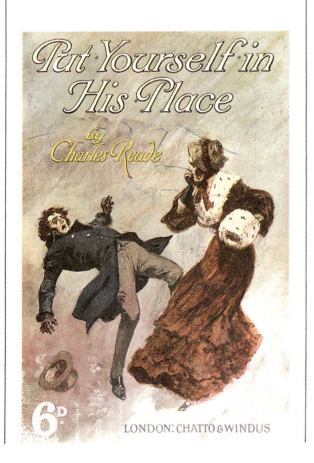

suffer. Even when faced with the murderous villains in **Rogues and Vagabonds**, the young couple keep their sense of proportion, fight their way through avaricious relatives, attempted murder, neglected children and wrongful imprisonment to a happy ending.

In more criminally-minded circles, Sims is also remembered for the creation of one of the first female detectives, Dorcas Dene, who unfortunately never appeared in the 6d. series.

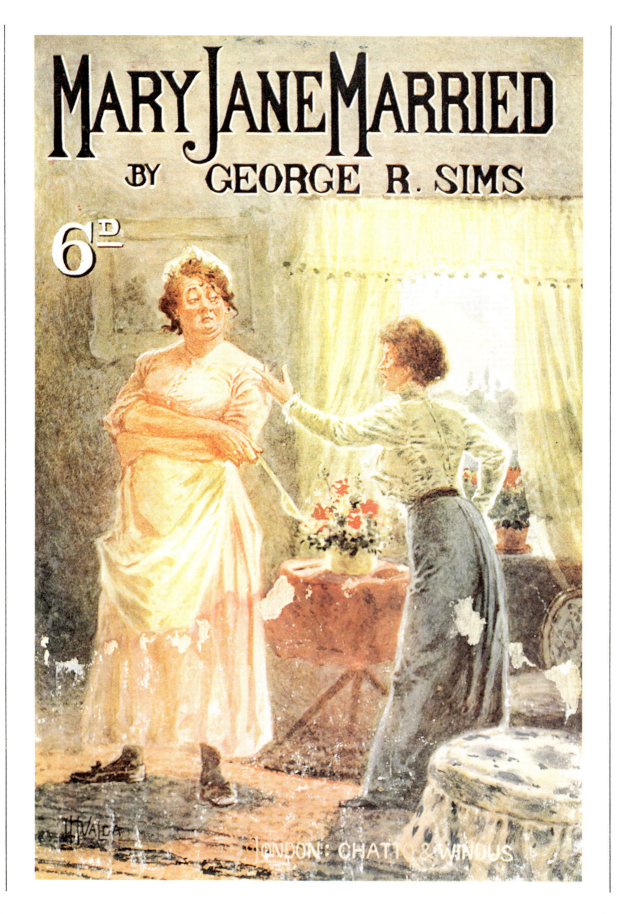

Men and Mystery

While women had a few champions, men had murder and mystery. Sir Arthur Conan Doyle (1859-1930) is so well known as the creator of Sherlock Holmes and Dr Watson that his other novels and romances are often forgotten. They are still readable and full of good stories and *The Exploits of Brigadier Gerard* has become very popular in the past decade as the horse named after the hero made his own reputation on the race course, a long way from Baker Street.

Conan Doyle's experience in the law and medicine stood him in good stead when he began writing, and most of his books are full of information garnered from both these professions, but in **The Firm of Girdlestone** the hero takes a more athletic interest than either Holmes or Watson would have been accustomed to.

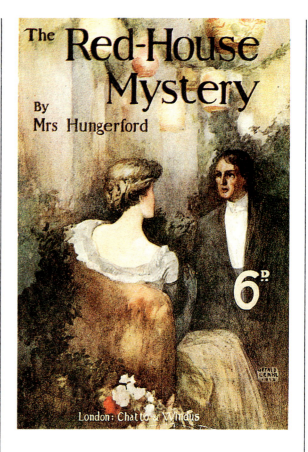

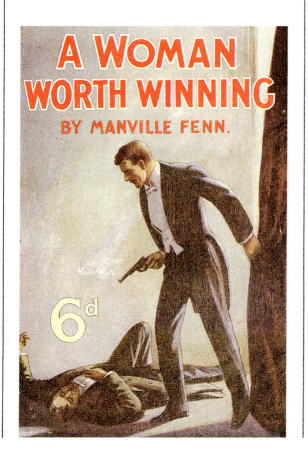

A Crimson Crime and **A Woman Worth Winning** are both perfect examples of *crime passionnel*, then an acceptable motive for murder, even if it was known by its French name, and was not quite the thing.

English crime writers adapted everything for their own use and began the long line of detective stories which was to become so distinctive a genre for women novelists from the 1930s on, while men have turned back to adventure and politics instead of pleasantly domestic murder.

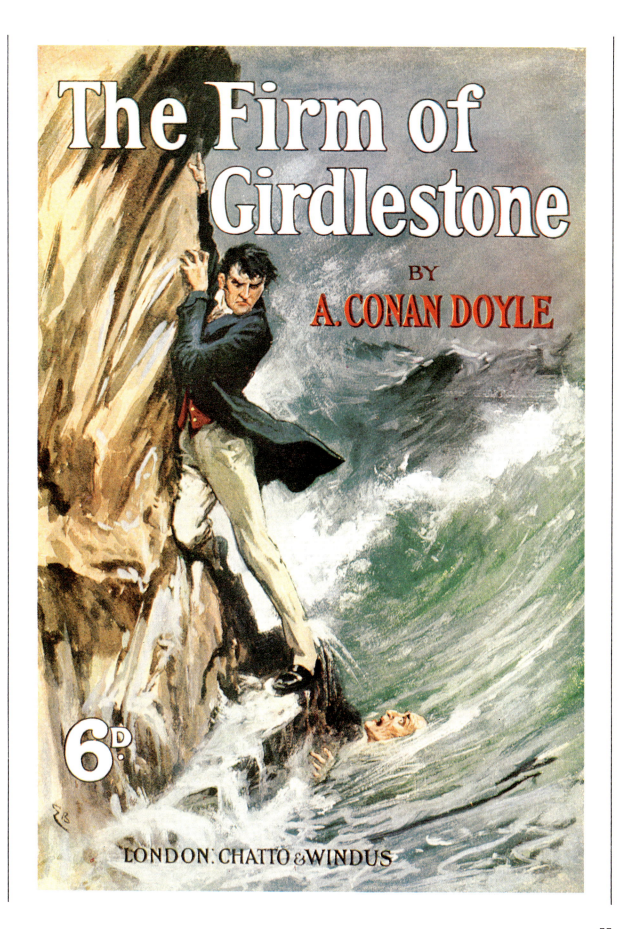

The Firm of Girdlestone

BY
A. CONAN DOYLE

6D.

LONDON. CHATTO & WINDUS

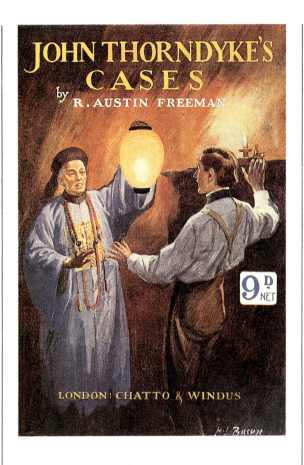

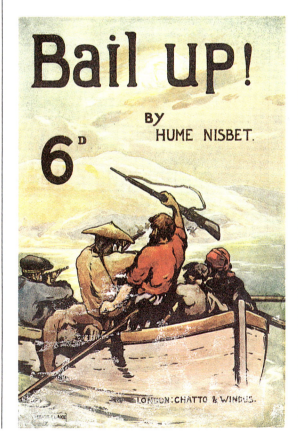

"Through the curtain he caught a glimpse of a dimly lit room; the rank sweet smell of opium was just distinguishable in the air. He could enter, but could he come out again? Would he come out again? . . . "

For the novelist trying to find something new and exotic, there was nothing better than the China and Japan of their imagination. Most oriental workers in the West stayed near the docks and the shipyards, and the glimpse of a pigtail was rare outside commercial neighbourhoods. Their language and customs made them easy to cast as villains and spies, but a decent Englishman in any story would always win, unless he was up against overwhelming odds. The gentleman on the cover of **By Proxy** only has three attackers – too few, perhaps, to qualify as a heroic struggle. Payn was a well-known editor, first at *Chambers Journal* after Dickens retired, and then at *The Cornhill Magazine*. Late in his career he turned to writing novels – only two were published in the series, and none of them remain in print. R. Austin Freeman (1862-1943) still has a fine reputation; he is best known among crime writers for the first real use of forensic medicine as part of his plots. Dr Thorndyke, the barrister and doctor protagonist of his novels, approved of his Chinese colleagues, as we can see from the pleasant and smiling face on the cover, which is a relief from the leering face of the stereotyped oriental at this period.

With **Bail Up** we are with the pirates on a mysterious southern sea – a coolie hat or two was enough to set the scene for the reader of desperate men shipwrecked off a rocky Asian coast.

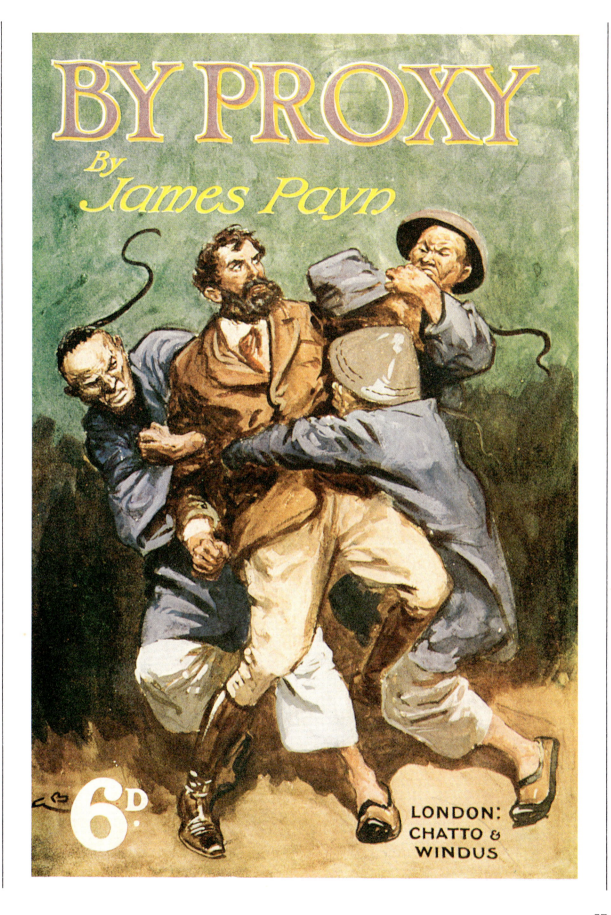

The Marseillaise

The French Revolution might have been started almost exclusively for the 6d. novel! It provided an endless source of elaborate thrilling plots for writers of every description on both sides of the Atlantic. Everything was woven into adventure – the suspicion of absolute monarchy, the glamour of the French court; the first triumph of democracy and the horrifying excesses of the following period; the romance of rescues by the Scarlet Pimpernel, and even the sexual lives of Napoleon and his wife.

Then, too, the indecency of French fashions were always good for a virtuous page or two of minute description, while the military genius of the Emperor could be admired with the comforting knowledge that sturdy British troops were to win the day after all at Waterloo.

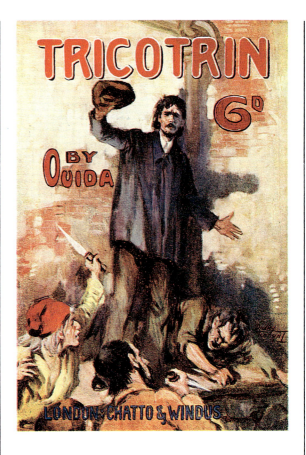

Perhaps it is not surprising that historical writers turned across the Channel so often. The English Civil War was still too raw a subject, the American Revolution perhaps too bitter a pill, and the rest of the world didn't really count. Here on the covers Napoleon fights his battles all over again, though why Mrs Massingham is so inimitable but so absent from the scene isn't quite clear.

Madame Sans Gêne was popular enough to be turned into an opera by Umberto Giordano in 1915; he had already achieved a personal triumph with "Andrea Chenier" in 1896, also based on incidents from the French Revolution.

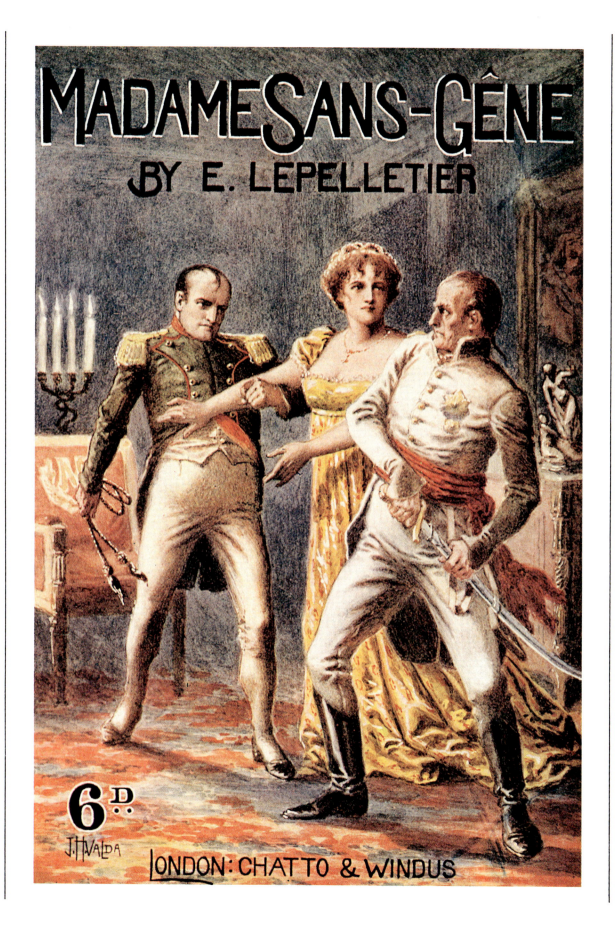

MADAME SANS-GÊNE

BY E. LEPELLETIER

6D..

J.H. VALDA

LONDON: CHATTO & WINDUS

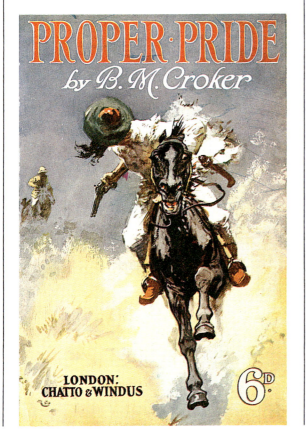

The New Empire

Around the turn of the century, the frontiers of the British Empire had settled down enough to make travelling possible for families, and visiting novelists. The predominantly rough and ready male society was becoming an overseas version of Home Counties family life. At the same time, the efforts and concerns of the social reformers who had focused on the problems in English society were now turned outwards towards India, the Middle East and Africa.

For many people at home, the new adventure novels were the only glimpse they would ever have of another land; for others, it was a guide to what to expect when they sailed across the globe. There was also enough adventure and excitement to create story after story: tribal battles, religious massacres, trading disputes, foreign spies, the wealth of native lands and the prospects of advancement.

Although most of the writers had lived or travelled in the countries they wrote about, the illustrators were less cosmopolitan as a whole. For the cover, it was enough to suggest a topee, a bit of tiger skin and a palm tree; only Bertram Mitford's illustrator made an attempt to portray real African warriors (with an English officer's hat, though). Mitford wrote three or four such adventures which were published to considerable approval from the press – "Mr Mitford convinces; he knows what it is to face the thundering hordes . . ."

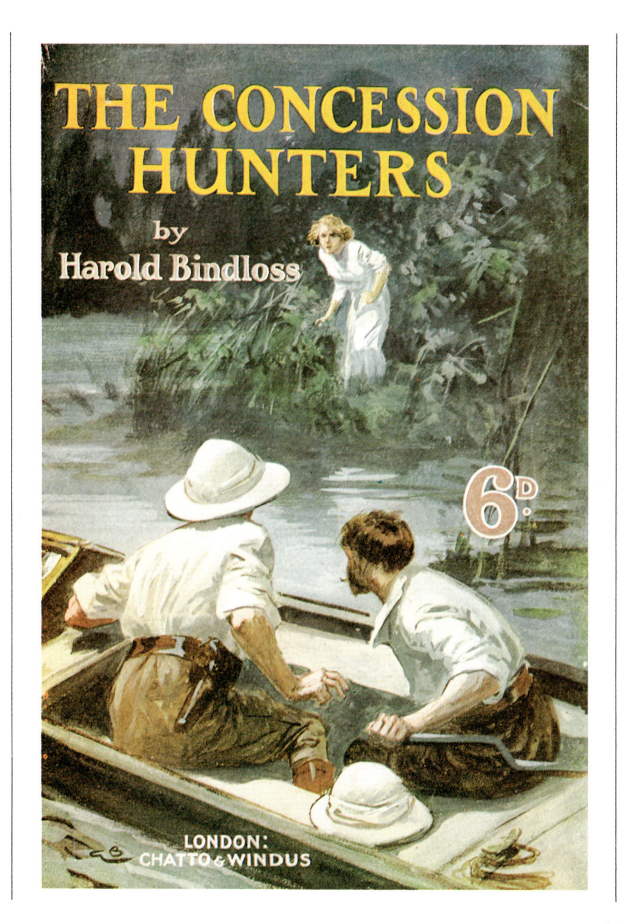

THE CONCESSION
HUNTERS

by

Harold Bindloss

6^{D.}

LONDON:
CHATTO & WINDUS

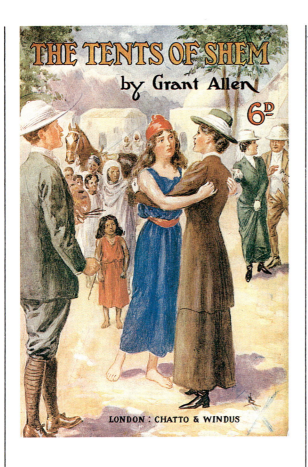

THE TENTS OF SHEM
by Grant Allen
6D
LONDON : CHATTO & WINDUS

PRETTY MISS NEVILLE
BY B. M. CROKER
LONDON : CHATTO & WINDUS

Among the Alien Corn

"Oh, William," she cried, "we *will* find a home out there, we will! We will!"

After the excitement of the journey from England to India and Africa, the heroines of these romances arrived with trepidation hidden under a surface of willing complaisance, just like their counterparts in real life. Many were as desperate to find husbands as the men were to find wives, and such transplanted couples usually tried to re-create the lives and the surroundings of their families 'back home'.

The women read voraciously finding solace in the new romances which could weave the life they saw around them into the familiar web of the English household. Novelists adapted their names and characters, learning to change the quiet gardens and village settings of earlier stories to more exotic places, just as Grant Allen (who had served in the Army) learned to make use of his own experiences in Africa.

But in spite of this knowledge the covers, painted in England of course, are full of curious anomalies; young ladies like **Pretty Miss Neville** were surely seldom accosted by tiger-skin bearers in the middle of the jungle, and it is difficult to understand what the illustrator of **A Family Likeness** thought would attract the reader.

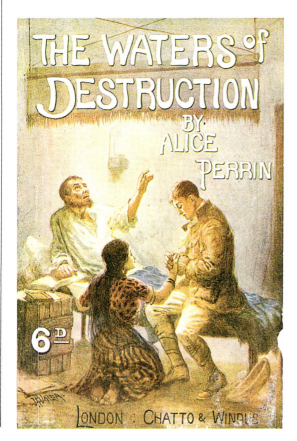

One of the strangest mysteries in the history of the 6d. novels is the disappearance of Alice Perrin from the history of 19th- and 20-century literature.

Mrs Perrin wrote at least seven titles for Chatto, mostly set in the East and particularly in India, which she knew and loved. Her depiction of native Indians and the problems of multi-racial marriage were remarkably unbiased for her period, and although she had many of the usual prejudices of the colonials, she was capable of seeing the real attractions of the Indian countryside as well as the damaging weaknesses of some British men and women who were totally unsuited to life in the Colonial service.

Her books gained astonishing acclaim from the press. *Punch* said she was often "second only to Kipling", the *Guardian* wrote, "She writes of what she knows, and what is much rarer, has the gift of communicating that knowledge . . ." "Among the English writers who have . . . been inspired by India . . . Mrs Perrin deserves a high place . . . she has drawn vivid, incisive sketches not only of Anglo-Indians but native life . . ." was part of an effusive review in *The Times*.

Perhaps today we might not be so blind to the omissions, the faults, and sometimes patronizing tone, but if Mrs Perrin had been writing about men, soldiers and battles instead of the domestic and romantic lives of her characters, she might still be in print, and her stories adapted for film and television.

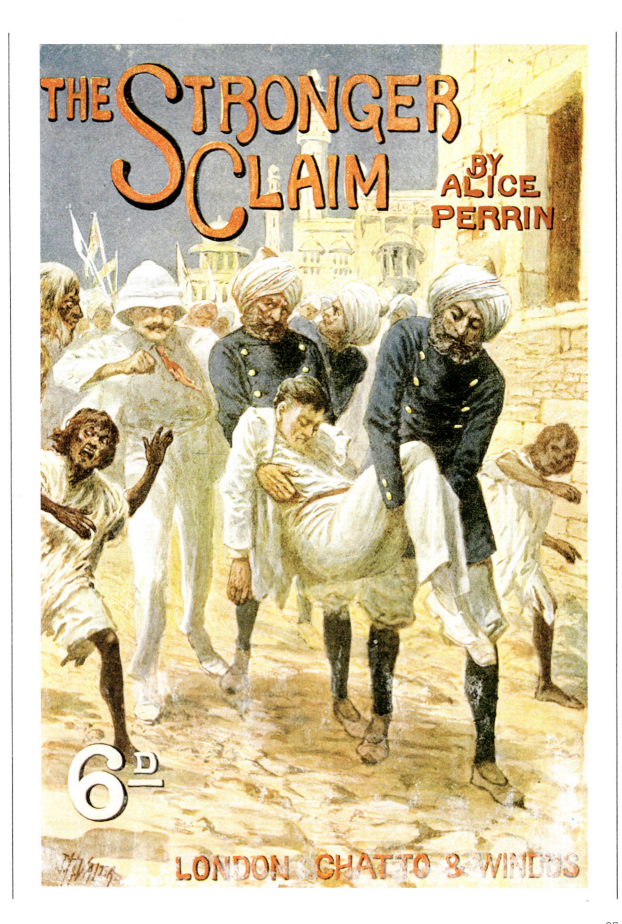

Pears Page

No Sixpenny Wonderful would have been complete without its Pears advertisement on the back cover. No matter how distraught the heroine, never mind how grim or frightening the scene, the reader had but to turn the book over, and all would be well. A Pears Baby was obviously cared for every minute of the day – loved, looked after, rosy-cheeked and full of mischievous laughter or appealing baby tears.

Sentimental, of course, but the advertisers knew a thing or two about human nature. Their precious bars of soap were natural partners for the novels, and as long as the series continued, the Pears Babies made sure there was a happy ending to every book.

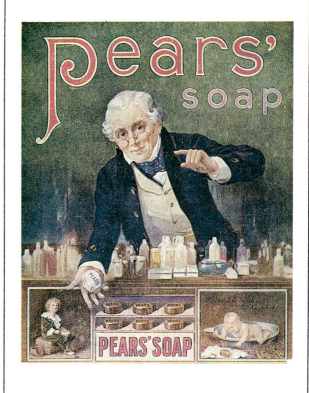

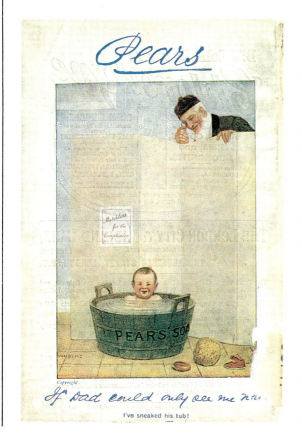

If Dad could only see me now.
I've sneaked his tub!

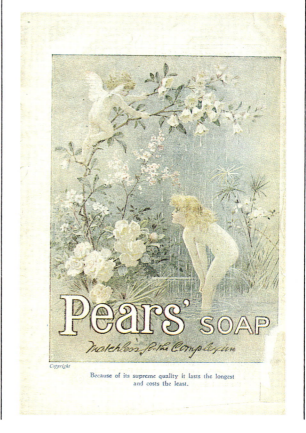

Because of its supreme quality it lasts the longest and costs the least.